Village cricket is the pu[...] [...]
national sport. All other [...] [...]
County cricket are m[...] [...]
wickets are flat and cl[...] [...]ts are
undulating, studded wit[...] [...]eeds and heavily
grassed. While first-class u[...]pires try to observe the laws of
cricket, village cricket umpires make their decisions in a
more arbitrary and, from the point of view of the sides they
represent, more sensible fashion.

Robert Holles has been an active member of his local village
team in Stebbing, Essex, for twenty-five years. Usually
batting at No. 10 or 11, he has had ample opportunity to
study the finer points of the game – the reluctance of
fielders to change sides between overs, the bottle of gin and
dry vermouth kept in the car to steady the nerves of a player
waiting to bat, the problems of grass-cutting and of
providing tea in an increasingly lazy world, and above all
pavilion politics. The full fruits of his experience are
presented in *The Guide to Real Village Cricket*.

Robert Holles was an Army sergeant in 1952 when his first novel, *Now Thrive the Armourers* (based on the exploits of The Gloucestershire Regiment in Korea) was published. Since then he has been a professional author and playwright, with eight novels, thirty television plays and a film to his credit. He is married, and lives in a sixteenth-century farmhouse at Stebbing, to which he recently returned after a year's stint as Artist-in-Residence at Central State University, Oklahoma.

Roy Raymonde received his training at the Harrow School of Art where he became increasingly influenced by the humorous approach to art and life inculcated by one of his teachers – the great Gerard Hoffnung. He became a full-time freelance cartoonist and humorist around 1960, since when he has gained an international reputation as a regular contributor to *Punch* and other magazines in London, to *Playboy* in America and Germany, and to a variety of publications in other parts of the world. Married, with two children, he lives in Essex not a stone's throw from the spot where many of the events in this book have taken place.

The Guide to Real VILLAGE CRICKET

Robert Holles

Illustrated by
Roy Raymonde

Foreword by
Trevor Bailey

London
UNWIN PAPERBACKS
Boston   Sydney

First published in Great Britain by Harrap Limited, 1983
First published by Unwin Paperbacks 1984

UNWIN ® PAPERBACKS
40 Museum Street, London WC1A 1LU, UK

Unwin Paperbacks
Park Lane, Hemel Hempstead, Herts HP2 4TE, UK

George Allen & Unwin Australia Pty Ltd
8 Napier Street, North Sydney, NSW 2060, Australia

Text © Robert Holles, 1983
Illustrations © Roy Raymonde, 1983

British Library Cataloguing in Publication Data

Holles, Robert
  The guide to real village cricket.
1. Cricket – England – Essex
2. Villages – England – Essex
I. Title II. Raymonde, Roy
796.35'8' 094267   GV928.G7
ISBN 0-04-796089-2

Set in 11 on 12 point Plantin by Fotographics (Bedford) Ltd,
and printed in Great Britain by Cox and Wyman Ltd, Reading

Foreword
BY TREVOR BAILEY

It has always been my belief that life without humour
would not be worth living, and that cricket without
humour certainly would not be worth playing. I am
therefore delighted to have been asked to write this
brief foreword for *The Guide to Real Village Cricket*
because it is a very funny book, which did not merely
make me chuckle, but had me laughing out loud on a
number of occasions.

Robert Holles, who originally acquired his place in
the Stebbing team by providing transport for away
matches, the captaincy by diabolical cunning, and the
No. 11 spot in the batting order on merit, has lived in
the village for twenty-five years. He describes with
relish and affection the ups and downs, which apply
to the game, performances, outfields, pitches and
administration. It is all there – the fun, the club
dinner, the AGM, the chicanery, a hilarious celebrity
match and very high-quality gamesmanship.

Born and bred in Essex, I am fortunate to know
Stebbing and their opponents, who come from places
with lovely names like Little Barfield, Hatfield
Heath, Kelvedon, Hatfield Broad Oak and
Tolleshunt D'Arcy. I also have great affection for the
cricket played in the rural north of the county, which
in its own particular way is as distinctive as that
provided by the Essex CCC. It is good to learn that
their brand of the game is still flourishing. It will, of

course, never bring them success in the Whitbread Cup, but they have avoided the menace of a fate worse than death, the commuter takeover, while none of them has yet become a phoney village eleven, like the one on the fringe of Epping Common, which Stebbing had the misfortune to encounter, and which despite the pseudonym I think I recognize.

The cartoons by Roy Raymonde simply enhance, complement and add another dimension to a delightful text.

Contents

Preface

Nobody would deny that village cricket is under threat, from attempts to modernize it, drag it shouting into the twentieth century, make it susceptible to changing fashions, even subject it to modern technology. I recently saw a scorer working out the bowling averages with a pocket calculator, and beside him an electronic scoreboard (which fortunately wasn't working!).

But the major peril has arisen from televised cricket, and the introduction of commercial sponsorship has introduced bizarre developments such as limited-over cricket, arbitrary field placings and the like. There is even a competition for village clubs on a nationwide scale with a final at Lord's – an almost obscene setting for a village cricket match.

It needs to be restated that village cricket is the pure and original manifestation of the game. All other forms, such as Test and County cricket, are bastardized offshoots, which must be considered in the light of splinter groups.

Thus any influences emanating from these flawed extensions of the real thing must be assiduously resisted. Parents have nothing to learn from their children.

It is in the hope of dispelling any confusion concerning what village cricket is all about that I present the following assessment of its character and personality, from my own twenty-five years' experience of the game, with all its complex philosophy and psychology.

I am not attempting to provide a set of rules – there aren't any. Although village cricket is loosely built around the laws of cricket, its adherence to them is subject to wide interpretations, and subtle variations, and is more characteristic in the breach than the observance.

Rather, I am hoping to provide a taste, a whiff of the essence of the game, which retired cricketers may recognize with nostalgia, and for which practising ones should prepare to give their lives, if necessary.

After all, we could survive without governments and leaders. But who would dare to suggest that we could live without village cricket?

Admission

The easiest way to get into a village cricket team is to be born the son of the farmer who owns the playing-field. It's also useful if you happen to be born in the village, and your father is already a regular and established member of the side – especially if he's the skipper. This can also have its own inbuilt disadvantage: if the father is a good cricketer, and the son merely useful or worse, he will find himself playing in the old boy's shadow for the next twenty-five years.

But if like myself one arrives on the scene at the age of thirty it can be much more difficult, particularly for a cricketer of my own modest pretensions.

The year was 1958, and I had one valuable asset – a car – which I was willing to place at the team's disposal for away matches. This vehicle, a 1938 Morris 8, stood up remarkably well to the burden of half a ton of cricketing flesh, together with a couple of Army kitbags full of gear, since at that time the club couldn't afford a proper bag. Had it once broken down, my tenuous hold on the No. 11 batting slot for away games would have been at serious risk.

During the first season I was only rarely picked for a home game. On these occasions the skipper would knock at my door about twenty minutes before the game was due to start. 'Er . . . Bob, would you like to

turn out for us today, only Peter's got a touch of the flu, and it's too late to find anyone else.'

But I had one further ace to play, a wife who was willing to do teas at frequent intervals. Once they had tasted her sausage rolls I was in for the home games as well. Thus it was that I finally became indispensable to Stebbing cricket, and a regular member of the side.

How to advise a modest performer on the techniques of admission in the current climate? Well, the car card's no use because everybody's got one. The tea card is useful, but not sufficient on its own.

There are other ploys, but they tend to be expensive, such as telling the club secretary that you have a strong connection with the sports-gear trade and can get anything the club needs at a 25 per cent discount. . . 'Oh, and by the way, if you happen to be a man short at any time . . .' Or you could say that you own a set of gang mowers and a tractor and would be happy to cut the outfield as and when necessary.

You then hire the necessary equipment, learn how to use it, and hope for the best. And if you have an attractive daughter who doesn't mind spending her Saturday afternoons selling raffle tickets, you are in with a chance.

Basic Composition

Village cricket teams are composed of two distinct elements – the gang of seven, and the gang of four.

The former group contains the first seven batsmen in the batting order, as well as all the bowlers, the wicketkeeper and the captain. The gang of four are the fielders, the umpires and scorers, the husbands of tea-ladies, outsiders looking in, perennially attempting to break into the select group of seven.

This is by no means easy. It is necessary, first of all, to prove one's usefulness to the team as a cricketer. But members of the lower quartet never get put on to bowl, and their chances of distinguishing themselves with the bat are few.

A batsman near the bottom of the order can often go without a knock for three or four games in succession, so that when he does get to the wicket he'll be sadly out of practice and over-anxious to make up for lost time.

And the occasion is seldom propitious. A gang-of-four batsman will usually find when he goes out to bat that there is only ten minutes to go before tea, his side has already made more than 150, and doesn't need his contribution anyway. Or the top batting will have collapsed to 35-7 after the opposition has notched 182, and the last three or four batsmen will be expected to make up the deficit in the final forty-five minutes, before stumps are drawn.

It is only very infrequently that a gang-of-four batsman will find himself in the position of affecting the result by knocking off the few runs needed for victory. This experience will prove so traumatic that he will inevitably fail, thus coming in for a rebuke from the skipper.

'Why didn't you just try and stay there, and let 'Arry get the runs? You'd got all the time in the world.'

A player who is once established as a member of the gang of seven is in much the same position as a docker: he has the job until he chooses to retire, and can then hand it over to his son.

When a vacancy does arise in this group, either by a member dying, or retiring, or moving to another district, he may be replaced by the longest-serving member of the gang of four, but this is not always the case. A cricketer from another village might recently have moved into the area, and if he is reasonably proficient with bat and ball he will immediately be accepted as gang-of-seven material, superseding any gang-of-four claimant.

The two-tier system acts as a buffer for the top tier. If one of the gang-of-seven members were to lose his batting form and gather a string of low scores he is protected from dropping too far down the order, and the lack of practice at both batting and bowling experienced by the lower four gives them no chance of posing a competitive threat.

There is also a steady turnover among the gang of four, as some members become discouraged at being on the fringe (or their wives rebel at making the teas once a fortnight) and they will drift away after some four or five years of continuous frustration. Yet there is never a vacancy for long – another hopeful will soon turn up and begin his long and usually fruitless apprenticeship.

My own membership of the gang of four lasted seven or eight years before I managed to break through to the seven through subterfuge – I contrived to snatch the captaincy by stealth. (See under Chairmanship.)

However, my elevation was strictly temporary, since I'd achieved it by unconstitutional methods. As soon as I lost the captaincy I was back at No. 11. And the way in which I lost it was entirely predictable. After my second year in the office, I felt confident enough to announce a new system. 'Everyone', I said, 'is going to get a fair crack of the whip.' For the rest of the season members of the gang of four found themselves occasionally opening the innings, even being put on for a spell of bowling. One or two of them rose to the occasion, others wilted under the pressure. Long-serving members of the gang of seven, finding themselves at No. 10 once every four or five games, came close to open rebellion.

It couldn't last – and it didn't.

Some cricketers in my experience have escaped from the gang of four in curious ways. One of them, Arthur, heard that a neighbouring village side was starting up again after being defunct for several years. He immediately offered his services as an experienced cricketer, was accepted, and has flourished as their wicketkeeper and opening batsman ever since. Another, Fred, turned up to watch a game for which he hadn't been picked. The opposition turned up one short and invited him to make up the number.

He persuaded them to give him a bowl, took five Stebbing wickets, followed by a brisk thirty runs. On the following Saturday he joined the gang of seven.

Desmond wasn't so lucky. Determined to break

out, he spent the winter training at the Essex County indoor nets. During the following season, batting at 10 or 11, he amassed 86 runs in 15 innings and was only three times out, finishing second in the batting averages.

Nobody was impressed.

Desmond sold his house and moved to Chignal Smealy.

Batting

There are two distinct varieties of batsmen in village cricket – those who can move their feet and get into a good position to play the ball (some 25 per cent), and those who can't. I have always belonged to the latter category.

Like the majority, I have been obliged to experiment with a wide variety of techniques to make up for this deficiency.

You start off by taking guard at middle and leg, as most professionals do, and repeatedly lose your off-stump. So you try middle and off, and qualify for lbw. You take guard a foot in front of the crease and get repeatedly yorked. You go back to a foot behind, playing off the back foot, and get caught behind the wicket. You change your grip on the bat-handle – it makes no difference. You increase your backlift as the bowler approaches, to no avail. The real problem is that there are too many ways of getting out. And whatever stance I took, there was always a gap of between six and eighteen inches between bat and pad whenever I made a stroke.

I found that if I could manage to survive a dozen balls I could usually make a few runs, but due to a serious and basic flaw in temperament I have nearly always taken a lunge at the third or fourth in a despairing attempt to get something against my name in the scorebook. And I have always attracted more than my share of unplayable balls, in particular those which pitch on a good length and then shoot across the sward as if held to it by an invisible magnet. I never encountered one of those that wasn't on the wicket.

For the first five years or so of my village cricket career the bowlers used to aim at the middle stump, and would not infrequently stray down the leg side, and it was during this period that I developed my one really effective scoring shot – a leg-pull. But this was at the time when colour TV was becoming commonplace in every drawing-room, and every detail of Test and county cricket matches minutely observed by the cameras. As a result, an obsession developed among bowlers to take a line just outside the off-stump, à la Truman, Snow, Lillee and Roberts, etc. This practice

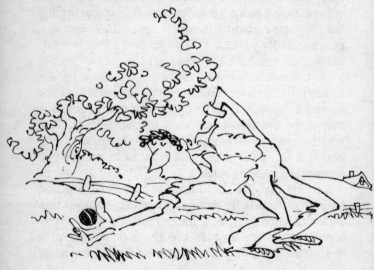

merely slowed the pace of the game – only about one wicket in forty in village cricket falls to a slip catch. But long-hops soon became a very rare luxury, and my best scoring shot was virtually eliminated overnight. I had to make do with clouts and slashes on the off-side, and thick edges to third man.

I've seen some interesting and original techniques practised by other batsmen. There was Phil, for instance, who always tucked his bat behind his front leg. He was frequently out leg before while he was still trying to disengage it.

Taffy had a strange tip-and-run sort of style. He would defend rigorously for three or four balls, then suddenly run five yards up the wicket, dab his bat on the approaching ball with a cry of 'Come on, then', and scamper to the other end. He finished his career with two records – one for running other batsmen out, and the other for getting seven consecutive ducks – the highest in the club's history.

Another batsman – I seem to remember that he played for Wickham Bishops – would crouch low, his bat at an angle of 45 degrees, both hands grabbing the handle from behind, stunning every ball for half a dozen overs. Then he would change his grip and stand up straight as a sapling. We knew he was ready to start making runs. He never did.

A romantic notion of village cricket is that of the local blacksmith smiting the bowling of the squire's son all over the park.

These days real blacksmiths are scarce, and seldom play anything more energetic than darts, and squires' sons spend their Saturday afternoons ripping out hedgerows and ploughing up public footpaths.

Yet genuine tonkers – those batsmen who instinctively get to the pitch of the ball, time their strokes perfectly, and send the ball soaring high and wide to the chapel roof, who can change the complexion of a game in a couple of overs – still exist, although they have become a rare species, their natural talents having been coached out of them by earnest P.E. teachers before they've had time to blossom.

Stebbing have possessed four genuine tonkers over the last twenty-five years – Big Tony, Bill – a Pakistani – Malc and Norman. The first two were built like armoured fighting vehicles, the second of steel cored wire. Bill once scored a hundred going in at No. 8, and I can recall him at Shalford clearing the players from the neighbouring tennis courts.

But like the mere plodders, tonkers normally require two or three overs to play themselves in, adjust to the bowling and the pace of the pitch, yet

14

since patience is seldom among their virtues, they frequently fall before they've got their eyes in. Malc, in one fraught period, collected five ducks on the trot, before restoring his average by belting a ton in twenty-five minutes.

Only Norman, a left-hander, seemed to function from the start. I once watched him collect 32 off the opening over, and he was the only batsman of my time who got 1,000 runs in a season.

Beer Matches

If a game finishes early – say before tea-time, one of the sides having been handed a hammering – a 'beer match' is organized between the two teams in order to whittle away the time until the pubs open.

It normally takes the form of a ten-over-a-side game, in which each player except the wicketkeeper bowls an over each. It is also customary for the batting order to be reversed, so that the gang-of-four batsmen at the bottom can be assured of getting a knock. However, this tradition never seems to have percolated through to the captains of Stebbing. I have played in numerous games involving a 'beer match' in which I did not get a knock at all, while all the members of the gang of seven had a couple.

There is usually a cursory attempt to keep the score, so that one team emerges as the victor, but nobody much cares – it's the result of the real game that matters.

Nor does the beer game offer much satisfaction to the players. Since the bowling is rubbish, there is no distinction to be had in smashing it all over the field, while it is all too easy to get out to a rubbish ball for nothing, so that when you walk back into the pavilion everyone looks the other way in embarrassment.

There are no set fields in beer matches. The fielders wander about haphazardly, usually around

the boundary, trying to find positions where a catch is likely to fall. Sometimes there is a change of wicket-keeper, but only if the regular one feels confident enough of his abilities to hand over the pads to another. Otherwise he will be extremely wary of some young player distinguishing himself behind the stumps and mounting a challenge for the future. No gang-of-four member is ever allowed to keep wicket, not even in a beer match.

Boundary

Where the long grass begins. Any attempt to mark it otherwise (white lines, pegs, etc.) should be firmly resisted.

Another deplorable feature which has recently crept into the village game – again, via the television set – is the habit of some batsmen of walking away from the crease as the bowler runs in, because someone (usually a toddler) is walking along the boundary behind the bowler's arm.

It would make no difference to the performance of the vast majority of village batsmen if a whole troupe of gorillas were permanently encamped there.

Bowling

Can be loosely classified as quickish, medium and slow. The quick can be fairly easily dismissed, since a genuine quickie arrives only once every fifteen years or so in a village cricket team, and is normally snaffled up in no time at all by the local town-team scout.

Stebbing only ever had one real quickie who stayed, in my experience. This was Malc, who was also a genuine tonker (see Batting).

Malc stood about five feet seven in his woollen socks as he began his vicious, curving little ten-yard run. He had a double-jointed wrist, and he would smack the ball down about a foot short of a length, and it would leap off the wicket, droning like a demented hornet. In a dry summer, on a bone-hard wicket, even the most dedicated of batsmen would be shuffling towards square leg as the ball was delivered, and the wicketkeeper would be halfway to the boundary.

Then there are, much more commonly, the pseudo-quickies, beefy young men in their early twenties with aggressive personalities, who try to use all their size and strength to bulldoze the batsman out. They tend to spray the stuff all over the place, gasping and sighing when the batsman plays and misses at a ball he cannot reach. But among the wides, full tosses and long hops they will just occasionally out of the blue, once every three or four overs, sling down a fast

19

swinging, squatting yorker right on the middle stump.

I was watching and waiting for just such a ball when facing the bowling of Maurice, a typical pseudo-quickie who played for Lindsell. Already I had tickled his full toss for a four behind the wicket, and got an easy couple past square leg from his attempted bouncer. I knew it was time for the swinging yorker.

Instead I got a murderous beamer straight out of an oak-tree behind the bowler's arm, which I only picked up when it was six inches from my teeth. I threw myself flat on the wicket. The ball dipped in a manner which defied every law of physics and smashed into the top inch of the leg-stump.

As I walked away Maurice called out, 'Sorry, Bob, it slipped out of my hand.'

One of Stebbing's pseudo-quickies was Trevor, a bellicose young man who approached his art with the finesse of an Aberdeen Angus in rut, even to the extent of pawing the ground when he began his 25-yard run. Playing against the Jolly Rogers, he opened the bowling and conceded 34 runs in three overs without taking a wicket – though having two catches dropped off stinging slashes – before he was taken off.

In the following game he bowled much more

steadily, and took three quick wickets in his opening spell. A fourth followed when the batsman cocked up a simple dolly to the captain, John, standing in the gully.

'You should have bowled like this last week, Trevor,' John said.

'Ar, and you should 'ave bloody caught like that last week!'

However, the greater part of a village side's bowling armoury is what might be termed the straight-up-and-down medium-paced stuff which relies on a good length and direction to restrict the runs, and the vagaries of the pitch allied to the uncertain temperament of the batsmen, to keep the wickets falling.

These medium-pacers, unlike the pseudo-quickies, are a patient breed of men who merely shake their heads when a simple catch goes down, or raise their eyebrows as a boundary shot races through a fielder's legs. Even when the patience is severely strained, the expostulations tend to be modest.

I recall an occasion when Herbie, one of Stebbing's long succession of straight-up-and-downers, was

bowling at a crucial point in a game with Rayne. Stebbing, batting first, had scored 87. The opposition were 83-9.

Herbie's bland features were screwed up with concentration. The first four balls of his over shaved the stumps of the Rayne No. 11, a last-minute choice who was wearing painters' trousers and sneakers with a Fair Isle sweater. He lunged at the fifth ball and it bobbled towards Arthur at square leg. The batsmen scampered a single and went for a suicidal second. But before they had crossed Arthur had pounced on the ball and flung it like a shell, some ten feet above the keeper's head. It rocketed, first bounce into a bed of thistles beyond the third-man boundary.

Herbie put his hands on his hips and glared across as the umpires removed the bails.

'Well, you might say suthen, Arthur,' he said. 'Even it that's only goodbye.'

Real slow bowlers, who can actually turn the ball, are regrettably becoming as rare in village cricket as mice in a skittle alley.

It takes a good deal of time and practice to develop the art of spin bowling, and considerably more cunning and artifice to persuade the skipper to give you any match practice. Since village cricketers are unused to spin bowling, the normal approach is to take a wild tonk at every third delivery, while attempting to block the other two, and in such circumstances it is nearly always the good-length ball which finishes up in the churchyard.

The only genuine tweaker who played for Stebbing in my time was Jack, the village greengrocer, who could regularly bring it in six inches from the off and bobble it around in flight somewhat. He got most of his wickets from the loose ones, but only ever got a bowl when everything else in the larder had been gorged, and regurgitated. He was always top of the bowling averages.

As with fast bowling, the genuine spinner has given way to the pseudo-tweaker, whose art has derived exclusively from watching the box.

They will begin by licking their fingers and flicking the ball from one hand to the other in the manner of

Abdul Qadir. They will then hide it, pressed against the small of their backs, as they commence their little curving, shuffling run, bowling around the wicket in order to appear suddenly and surprisingly from behind the umpire. They deliver with a sort of skipping cartwheel action, lobbing the ball high in the general direction of the wicket.

The batsmen will at first be suspicious, watching and waiting for the turn. When they realize that there is no spin on the ball they will begin to react accordingly, and with enthusiasm.

Yet it is not unusual for a pseudo-tweaker to pick up a vital wicket, as on the occasion when I saw one of ours toss a ball so high to the opposition's star batsman that it passed a yard over his head. The batsman – an egocentric fellow with a crisp ginger beard and a fashionably ragged sun-hat – raised his bat like a tennis racket and took a contemptuous flick at it. The ball glanced off the bottom into the wicketkeeper's hands.

My own career as a bowler was inauspicious. Bowlers need to be invited by the skipper to bowl if they are to get any bowling practice. I did occasionally get an over (along with every other player) in a beer match, and on these rare occasions I experimented with a wide variety of techniques, around six in the course of an over. I might start with a medium-pacer of flat trajectory bowled with a round-arm action – which an alert umpire might have called for chucking. The next one would have a bit of top spin on it in the hope that it would skid through (it never did!) and I would try to confuse the batsmen by bowling from the edge of the crease and around the wicket and mixing in a couple of pseudo-tweakers. I would sometimes take a wicket, but in beer matches it doesn't count.

There was one occasion, against Lindsell, when I was actually put on to bowl in a real match.

The opposition were batting first. It was getting near tea-time, they were about 170-5, one of the openers had just got his hundred, seven bowlers had already been tried, when the skipper tossed the ball to me.

I began bowling at a batsman who had just come in. He took a four off my second ball, so I decided to upset his concentration by coming round the wicket. The batsman was a farm-worker who spent most of his working life astride a tractor seat, and there was a large gap between his knees. My next ball went straight through the middle of it and rapped the furniture.

Shortly afterwards I found myself facing the opener. There was no gap between his legs, and he advanced to 150 in no time at all.

Captaincy

If you were to ask a representative of almost any profession – policemen, nurses, politicians, prostitutes, tailors, greengrocers, stockbrokers, bookmakers, etc – what were the essential qualities of their calling, they would almost certainly say honesty, integrity and a sense of humour.

In a good village cricket captain these qualities would be utterly redundant. He would be much better equipped with cunning, deceitfulness and hollow cynicism, not to mention a basic appreciation of the complexities and fluctuating psychological patterns of the game.

His temper is also important. He should not be too bossy or fussily meticulous, but on the other hand he should be firm, and not incapable of losing his temper with slovenly fielders who are seen to be hugging cats near the fine-leg boundary when a thick edge is ballooning towards them, or wayward batsmen who get bowled trying to hook a yorker.

I am compelled to admit that during my association with the Stebbing Cricket Club the majority of skippers (excluding myself, of course) have appeared to be seriously lacking in a grasp of the fundamentals.

The captaincy begins with tossing a coin. The winning captain has the choice of batting first or second. The advantages of batting first are as follows:

26

The team which bats first has some twenty minutes more batting time than the team which bats second. It also has first use of the wicket, which is likely to be scarred and battered when the team batting second is batting. Also, the team batting second has the worst of the light, and if it is late on in the season can easily finish in pitch-darkness.

Furthermore, if the team batting first gets a useful score – anything over 120 – the team batting second will inevitably be demoralized, especially when it gets past pub-opening time, and will almost certainly be crushed.

Yet I have known innumerable occasions when a Stebbing skipper (apart from myself, of course) has put the opposition in to bat. Abject reasons are given for this decision.

'Well, the wicket's had a bit o' rain on it this mornin', so I rec'n that oughter be a bit lively.'

'Well, there's a lot o' low cloud about, so I reckon ol' Charlie oughter be able to swing it about a bit.'

'Well, they ain't a very strong side, so I rec'n we oughter try'n make a game of it.'

Inevitably the wicket isn't so much lively as limp as soft putty, Charlie doesn't manage to swing it an inch out of line, and the weak side, encouraged by their astonishing luck in having been put in to bat, give us a sound thrashing.

Placing the field is admittedly a difficult operation for a captain.

The classic fielding positions – third man, point, slips, cover point, extra cover, mid-off, mid-on, mid-wicket, square leg, fine leg, etc – have been developed over the centuries to cover the scoring shots of batsmen of county standard.

But village cricketers do not possess in their rustic armoury shots like square cuts, cover drives, hooks, sweeps and glances. They make their runs by virtue of dabs, tickles, nudges, thick and thin edges, pulls, clouts and slogs which are inclined to go just about anywhere, except in the direction of the conventional field placings. So the skipper must set his field by instinct, by hand-waving and wagging, Archie could you go just a bit deeper and round to the right a bit . . . and adjust it periodically according to the batsmen's strengths and the bowlers' weaknesses. A man on the square-leg boundary is always a good idea, as is another at fine enough leg to double as long stop. Numerous village cricket games are won and lost through an excess of avoidable extras.

The nature of the playing-field should also be taken into account. If it is on the side of a hill with a twenty-foot drop from one side to another at least eight fielders should be posted on the downhill side, whichever end the bowling is coming from.

Skippers must also be cognizant of the reluctance of fielders to change sides between overs. What usually happens is that square leg and cover point will gesture to each other, and each will move a yard to the left.

It becomes even more complicated when a left-hander is batting. A skipper who loses touch with events for an over or two will find that he's got three leg-slips and five men in the covers.

Village cricket captains also tend to be frequently and adversely affected by television viewing.

In normal circumstances a cricket ball (nowadays rather expensive) will be required to last for three games. But many skippers, when the other side bats first, will decide to use a new ball, the theory being that their opening bowlers will be able to make use of the shine to 'swing it around a bit'.

The truth of the matter is that a village side will be lucky if it finds a genuine swing bowler more than once in a generation, and when they do he will be swiftly snapped up by the Gentlemen of Essex, after a quick obligatory course in speech therapy designed to obliterate any trace of an Essex accent.

The end-result is that by the end of the season there is a surplus of once-used balls, and a heavy expenditure on Cherry Blossom oxblood polish in preparation for the following one.

In village cricket the wickets are always undulating, usually heavily grassed, sometimes studded with weeds, and always open to the weather. Any ball bowled, whether hard or soft, dull or shiny, round or oval, is likely to rear, squat, move, swerve, or sit up and beg arbitrarily, whoever happens to be bowling it.

In one game against Castle Hedingham we took the first three wickets cheaply – and then their tonker came in. The ball was a new one, but in the first over he put it into a bed of brambles at deep mid-wicket. Four other balls of various vintage followed – two in the duckpond, two more in the elephant grass growing around the chapel tombstones. Finally we produced our last remaining ball. It was as soft as a pillow, with the insides bulging through the seam. The tonker was through his stroke before it was halfway up the

29

wicket, and it bowled him. The rest of the batsmen fell in similar fashion, well before tea-time. But during the tea interval the new ball was discovered and reclaimed, and we marched on to a handsome victory.

One of the major arts of captaincy is knowing when to change the bowling. All too often the average skipper is deficient in this important tactic.

The usual idea is to start with your two regular openers – the quickest ones – and keep them on for a dozen overs or more, whether they are taking wickets or not. They are then replaced by change bowlers, inevitably a pair of straight-up-and-downers lacking length, line and direction as well as pace, who provide a welcome respite for the batsmen.

In my first game as skipper I decided to break the mould. We were playing Little Bardfield – a local derby. They went in first, and their first three wickets went down cheaply. But then a stubborn pair got together, put on about thirty, and were beginning to look dangerous. So I took off one of the openers and tossed the ball to John, who had never bowled before except in a beer match. He sent down an unpredictable assortment of high lobs and long hops. In his first over both batsmen cocked up simple catches.

I then took him off, and the regular bowlers finished off the rest of the batsmen quickly, demoralization having set in. We won the game comfortably.

I have to admit that when I tried to repeat this tactic against Kelvedon, a few weeks later, John was thrashed for about 25 off his single over, and no wickets fell. Which proves, if anything, that the game is more susceptible to luck than inspired judgment, although it is essential for a good captain to keep using his imagination. If the game is won he claims the credit; if lost, its the fault of the gods, as expressed during the inquest in the pub afterwards.

'I rec'n we was dead unlucky. If only Derek 'ad managed to cling on to that catch when they was 37 for 5 . . .'

'That feller with the beard that got forty-odd . . . talk about a charmed life . . .'

'That openin' bowler o' theirs . . . should 'ave been no-balled every time . . .'

'Keith should never 'ave been given out. That was a bumped ball.'

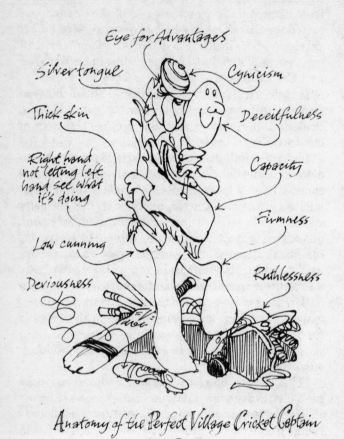

Eye for Advantages

Silver tongue

Cynicism

Thick skin

Deceitfulness

Right hand not letting left hand see what it's doing

Capacity

Low cunning

Firmness

Deviousness

Ruthlessness

Anatomy of the Perfect Village Cricket Captain

Chairmanship

After I'd been playing for Stebbing for five years or so I was surprisingly elected chairman.

This is a rather ambiguous position in village cricket. The chairman is required to run the committee meetings, and do the waffling at the annual dinner, as well as find the principal speaker for that event. This last obligation is perhaps the most difficult which attends the office. I would normally start about six weeks ahead of time with an invitation to someone like Bernard Miles. I would receive his secretary's expression of regret some three weeks later. I would then try the Essex County Cricket Club. Keith Fletcher already has another engagement. Also Ray East. Trevor Bailey? Out of the country. With ten days to go I try the local Round Table, who suggest a Coggeshall farmer who is much in demand and can also play the guitar. He is available, but wants sixty quid.

Three days to go. I finish up with a vicar from three parishes distant, who insists on saying grace before we all attack the vegetable soup. His anecdotes are limp.

Old Jim, who has brought his own supply of rum and blackcurrant, hectors and harangues the speakers, shouting at them to speak up, asking the vicar if he calls himself a Christian. Someone leads him out to be sick, and in due course he starts all over

again. His incessant cry, 'You don't know what you're bloody talking about,' is directed at every speaker, including the secretary, who is annotating last season's results from the scorebook.

There is afterwards a dance. A live band is not to be afforded, but there is a disco Johnny from Lindsell, himself the other side of fifty, who tries to strike a balance between young and old. A mixture of Rolling Stones, the Hokey-Cokey, Dashing White Sergeant, Chubby Checker, and Victor Sylvester. As chairman I am obliged to request the sound to be reduced on several occasions, since Johnny Disco keeps retiring to the bar and his shock-haired assistant turns it back to ear-bursting pitch again.

Since the Scout hut where the function is held lacks sufficient space, the bar itself is squashed into a narrow corner. Various cricketers are on duty behind it for about an hour apiece, and I have craftily arranged my own stint just after the end of the dinner, so that I'm not too stoned to count the change. Also, I hope to keep an eye on things later. But they seem to pass by. It is others who tell me the following morning that six or seven local yobbos tried to gatecrash at half-eleven, and Derek threw one of them over the palings into Mrs Ackroyd's garden.

After the dinner the speaking vicar retires quickly. There is stomping and shouting and the fug of cigarette smoke and chalk dust and the announcement of winning raffle tickets has to be screamed over the microphone, across the buzz of drunken men making propositions to the wives of other drunken men which they have neither the intention, nor capacity, to support, while hugging them on the dance floor. At the end of the evening there are just four of us left, glassy-eyed survivors intent on locking up and seeing that the money is safe. We collect together again, at about midday on the following morning – a Sunday – to clear up, fold up the chairs and stack them, discuss the events of the preceding night, wash up the glasses, and collect our perks, a division of the booze which is left over.

For a while after my elevation to the chairmanship I held the committee meetings for convenience in the front room of my cottage, until I made the mistake of asking the members to assist in shifting a piano down a narrow staircase. This was accomplished with grunting good humour, but I was later made aware of a strong groundswell of opinion in favour of holding future meetings in the saloon bar of the King's Head.

At the start of my term of office the cricket-club buildings consisted of a couple of white-painted toolsheds, where the teams changed among the rat-droppings, broken stumps and garden tools, draping their jackets on the handles of clapped-out lawnmowers. I decided to change all this. A large construction workers' hut was found and bought, and taken to the ground in sections. This flurry of activity seemed to have exhausted the members, and the sections lay there all through the winter and well into the following spring. It was about mid-April that I decided to make a move, and began laying the brick piers single-handed.

This produced an immediate reaction. Several team-members – carpenters, bricklayers, plumbers – would turn up to watch and make critical assessments concerning the quality of the work. 'If you think you can do it better, what's stopping you?' I inquired.

Though disgruntled and reluctant, they got the message, and decided to make a serious effort. The new pavilion was raised in a fortnight, and painted inside and out within the month.

But I was to suffer for this importunity. Jeff, the skipper for the ensuing season, gave me a permanent slot in the batting order – No. 11. During that season I did a great deal of fielding, and almost forgot what it was like to hold a bat.

After three games running without getting a knock I decided to make my protest at the next opportunity, a home game against Estuary Amblers.

Before the game started the opposing captain approached Jeff with a not unusual request. 'We've got a spare man with us,' he said. 'Can we make it twelve a side?'

Jeff agreed, and called to a nine-year-old boy who was imprinting his muddy signature on the wall of the tea-hut by kicking a football against it. 'Ey, Peter, would you like to play for us today?'

Peter intimated that he would be delighted.

'Well, you get off home and pick up your whites and I'll give you a game.'

As the ecstatic youth pelted home on his bike Jeff went out to spin the coin. He returned, announced that we were batting first, and started to write down the batting order. I peered over his shoulder as the names went down. Peter was in at No. 11; I was No. 12.

37

I decided it was now or never.

'Er, Jeff . . . excuse me a minute, but . . .'

He glanced up. 'Oh there you are, Bob. I been lookin' for you. Would you like to go out and umpire for a little while?'

It was at this juncture that I realized there was an essential element missing from the office of chairman: a modicum of pure, naked power. I decided to adjust the situation as soon as I could.

The opportunity arose at the following annual general meeting, which took place on a bleak evening in early March. A few days earlier I had taken aside a couple of fellow-members of the gang of four, Eddie and Vic.

'Look,' I said, 'you blokes are always stuck at the bottom of the order. The skipper never gives you a chance to get a decent knock together. Isn't that right?'

'Right!'

'Well, I'd like to do something about it . . . with a little help from my friends . . .'

The AGM was as usual rather thinly attended – about a dozen were slumped around in their duffle coats and anoraks as I opened the proceedings. The secretary's report, the treasurer's accounts, passed without incident. It was now time for the election of officers. I was quickly confirmed in my own office, there being no competition of any kind, as were the secretary and the treasurer. Next, the captains.

There were two at this time, one for Saturday games, the other for Sunday's. The two skippers of the previous season were proposed.

There is a tradition in village cricket that captains

must affect to show the same sort of reluctance to accept office as the Speaker of the House of Commons. The two skippers in this case reacted according to custom.

'Well, I don't know. I got a lot o' work on this year. I don't think I'll 'ave time.'

'Well, I been skipper now for the last five year . . . I rec'n that's about time someone else took a turn.'

'Any other proposals?' I inquired.

Eddie's voice rose from a fug of low-tar content.

' 'Ow about you, Mr Chairman?'

I appeared to consider this proposal gravely, then waved a deprecating hand.

'Well, as no one else seems to be willing, I'll be prepared to take it on for Saturdays.'

'I'll second that proposal,' grunted Vic from behind his pint of Adnams.

'Anyone against?' I asked.

There was a pindrop silence.

'Right, any more nominations for the Sunday captain?'

Changing-rooms

Time was when all changing-rooms were clapboard huts the size of chicken-houses with wooden benches and six-inch nails for pegs. After the game they would be filled with sweaty camaraderie and flying jock-straps, as the cricketers jostled and fought to identify their clothes. The only decoration would be a nudie bookmaker's calendar, and a dog-eared list of those who still hadn't paid their subs since the season before last.

But a gradual change has been taking place. Changing-rooms now reek of pinetree-smelling talc and deodorants. The benches have been flogged to antique dealers. There is room to move. In certain deplorable cases some interfering local council has stepped in with a substantial grant, and there will be stainless-steel lockers and shower-rooms and porcelain toilets – even electric lighting. And there will be a grizzled caretaker lurking around to 'keep an eye on things'.

My favourite changing-rooms remain the ones at Kelvedon and Little Bardfield. At Kelvedon a long shutter runs along the length of the building, and this is always propped wide open, the hooks and eyes have long since solidified with rust, so that one undresses in full view of passing ladies, at the mercy of the prevailing weather conditions. The one at Little

Bardfield also doubles as tea-hut and equipment store, so that shirts and slacks are draped over the handles of rusting motor-mowers, socks tucked into discarded kettles.

There is another, at a village near Sawbridgeworth, which was a wartime air-raid shelter: a dank and windowless concrete tomb, with ranks of rusting lockers at one end which nobody dared to open. They were probably full of rotting gas capes and respirators.

Clowns

Many village sides have a resident clown.

This functionary requires the attributes of a caustic (but not too erudite) wit, a laugh like a prairie dog with croup, and a loud and penetrating voice, so that insults bawled from the pavilion balcony can be heard clearly on the pitch:

'Give that man a bucket!'

'Ey, Biggsy, you're not supposed to be the night-watchman, y'know!'

Or when a batsman is writhing in pain on the ground:

'Watch 'im, umpire. 'E's playin' for time.'

Or to an incoming batsman who has just had his stumps spreadeagled: 'Did they give you out, Norman? I didn't 'ear anyone appeal.'

But like circus clowns, the village cricket variety exude an element of pathos, even during their best performances. They are never good cricketers, since good cricketers always take themselves seriously, and they owe their inclusion in the team to their capacity to amuse and entertain the other players, and even more so to act as the team butt, and recipient of counter-insults, to which they are all too vulnerable. Clowns are invariably members of the gang of four, never batting above No. 8, and only getting to bowl the odd over during a beer match.

Let me describe a typical village-cricket clown . . . call him Porky . . . a seventeen-stone, balding man in his late thirties who emerged in the indeterminate past from the North London suburbs.

Ten years earlier he was a useful rugby forward with Bishop's Stortford, but time and wind have taken their toll, he has descended through the teams to the third, fourth and finally the Extra B. At this point Porky, deciding to move on to gentler pursuits, attaches himself to the nearest village cricket team.

After some years of batting in the depths of the order, Porky manages to develop a technique of some sort. He stands in front of his wicket like a Buddhist monument, trying to prod every ball a foot in front of his anchored feet. Despite his size and strength, he has no backlift or follow-through, and the rare boundaries he collects come off the edge. There is only one trophy that he collects at the annual dinner, all too frequently. This is a Victorian porcelain bed-pan – the Mallard Trophy – which is awarded to the batsman who records the highest number of ducks during the season.

Occasionally he tries, and sometimes succeeds, in proving his usefulness by hanging on for two or three overs at the end of the innings while his partner attempts to score the winning runs.

Most of Porky's cricketing life is spent, of course, fielding or umpiring. In the field (where he is only marginally more mobile than a tank-trap) he will take up a position fairly close to the wicket, such as shortish mid-on. Of the catches which come his way, he will hang on to about one in four, but will manage to make all of them look incredibly difficult, sprawling sideways as the ball bounces off his chest, or flapping his wrist with a grimace of simulated agony as it bobbles out of his hands. Perhaps once every two or three seasons he will manage to hold two catches in the course of a single match. This feat will be talked about incessantly for the rest of the season, by Porky.

But it's in the pub afterwards that he really comes to life and performs his true function. Porky can not only hold his liquor, he can consume more of it over a shorter period than any of his team-mates. If one

player has made over fifty runs or taken more than five wickets during the game he will traditionally fill a jug of ale and pass it round. Porky will have sunk his first pint while the others are still waiting for the froth to settle on theirs.

It is now that Porky conducts his personal inquest into the game, punctuated by his special brand of personal comment:

' 'Course you was out lbw. I could see it from where I was sitting. Well, I mean, if you insist on tryin' to stop the ball with your knackers, what more d'you expect?'

'Fast? 'Ow do you know 'e was fast? You were shuttin' yer eyes every time 'e ran up to the wicket.'

'I'm surprised you got fifty, with your bloody luck. You was dropped five times, and you ran at least four other blokes out. I suppose you wanted to make sure they didn't get more runs than you did.'

But his sharpest sallies are reserved for those few members of the team who are older than himself – it is almost as if Porky hates and fears the ageing process

more than age itself:

' 'Allo, Granddad . . . what was the matter with you today? Did you forget to take your Phyllosan?'

' 'Ere, give us another pint of Newcastle Brown . . . and stick one in the box for my father.'

'You still 'ere, Arthur? Did your nurse give you a special extension?'

But there are no easy victims. The elders return the jibes with interest.

'Porky, when was the last time you made a stand?

Or can't you remember?'

'Ey, Porky, if you got as many runs as you dropped catches, you'd double your average.'

'Er . . . Porky . . . I've got your Preparation H in the car. You left it in the changin'-room.'

'Looks as if you'll 'ave to go 'ungry next week, mate. The Meals on Wheels is on strike.'

'Did you get any runs today, Porky? I was lightin' a fag while you was in, so I didn't notice.'

Thus Porky continues, as the seasons pass. Eventually the club presents him with the Mallard Trophy, since he has won it so many times.

He creeps towards the middle forties, and is finally confronted with a disastrous situation. The last of the elders retires from the game. Porky has become the team grandfather himself.

Faced with a few more years of self-mockery, he decides to go into semi-retirement, announcing that he will only be playing the 'odd game' in future. But the skipper doesn't pick him for any game whatsoever.

Porky thinks about taking up golf. Perhaps there's a vacancy for a resident clown in the clubhouse.

But not bowls, of course. Bowls is an old man's game.

Commuter Takeovers

During the last twenty-five years, along with the commuter explosions in the big conurbations, the infiltration and takeover of village cricket clubs within an ever-widening radius has spread like a vile fungus. In the South-East area, for instance, village teams as far from London as North Essex and South Oxfordshire have succumbed, and many others are in imminent peril.

It begins like this. At the pub session after a home game a suave stranger will introduce himself to the

club secretary, buy him a pint, and begin to chat affably and knowledgeably about cricket. He will let it drop that he has recently moved into the village from some suburb like Chigwell and wouldn't actually mind the odd game for the village side if he can be fitted in. He'll admit that he's a bit out of touch at the moment, adding that he used to have the 'odd game' with the Bank of England Wanderers.

The secretary, suitably impressed, will make a mental note and the stranger will say, 'Look, why don't you call me Adrian?' and will write down his telephone number for the secretary in case the mental note fails to stick.

A few weeks later Adrian will make his first appearance for the village team, going in No. 5 and knocking up a steady if undramatic thirty or so, apologizing later for getting out to a rash stroke. A few weeks later he will be batting at No. 3, and opening the bowling. In the following season he will be elected skipper.

Within two years there will be two or three others like Adrian playing for the village, and after five, seven or eight. The takeover will be virtually complete.

By this time there will be sight-screens behind the wickets, and the roller will be used between innings. The resemblance to real village cricket will be remote, and anybody who was born and bred in the place who wants a game of cricket will have to whistle for it.

These commuter-predators are not too difficult to identify. They have names like Julian, Jeremy, Charles, Martin. They earn their living in areas such as banking, insurance, public relations and run Jaguars, Rovers, Volvos. When playing cricket they arrive with personal cricket bags bearing their initials in gilt, and their caps are fashioned in a series of thin concentric rings. Their wives are seldom if ever seen doing their stuff in the tea-hut.

Elderly Players

One of the great advantages of village cricket is that it is more of a psychological conflict than a physical one, so that most players (assuming they retain a modicum of health and fitness) can continue to perform until they reach their fifties.

There are a few who continue well beyond this accepted limit. I recall one old boy – a county player in his time – who was still turning out in his mid-seventies.

He would come out to bat, reeking of menthol, and meticulously take guard after carefully prodding the

pitch. As the bowler began his run in this veteran would begin to wind himself up like a clockwork armadillo. He would achieve maximum backlift and be moving into his stroke as the ball left the bowler's hand. He always struck the ball somewhere near the middle of the bat, usually working it away for a leisurely single. He once sneaked about 76 in this fashion during a couple of frustrating hours, then departed, shedding his gloves and groping in his pocket for his teeth.

Another ancient regularly opened the batting for Wendens Ambo, and was as hard to shift as a concrete bus-drivers' toilet. After nudging and scraping a half-century he proudly announced in the tea-hut that he was celebrating his fiftieth year in village cricket. As we crunched into the cucumber we fervently hoped that he would decide to call it a day.

Equipment

In the present era of relative affluence the great majority of village cricketers wear whites. Twenty years ago it was not unusual for players to take to the field in bib and brace overalls. A heavy sweater is recommended for the English climate, and a good one can last for a hundred years, and be handed down to several generations of cricketers.

The old peaked schoolboy cap, displaying the club's colours and badge, is now almost entirely out of fashion, giving way to the floppy white sun-hat – another television innovation – and occasional oddities such as American baseball caps or the sort of headgear more commonly worn by Dutch bargees.

Pads and gloves are of course essential, and many players use their own bats, which tend to become highly personal to the owner, oiled and bound with loving care, but sometimes roundly chastised, even hurled across the changing-room after failing to deliver the goods.

For any player wishing to preserve his sexual capacity, a box is obligatory. As a young player, fearless and confident, I used to bat without one, until I found myself writhing on the turf after contact with a ball of modest pace.

In the pavilion afterwards an old, knowledgeable

cricketer with a complexion of fumed oak took me aside.

'I should always wear a box if I was you, mate,' he warned. 'An old friend o' mine, 'e never used to wear

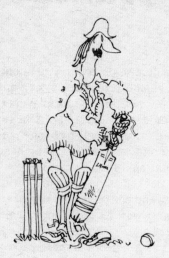

one either, and 'e copped a real snorter. They swelled up to the size o' coconuts arter.

'That was a couple o' years ago, and 'e still has ter go to 'orspital once a fortnight to get the fluid drained off.'

I followed his advice.

Fielding

This is a subject on which any gang-of-four member has to be an acknowledged expert, since it will consume at least 50 per cent of his cricketing life. The other 50 per cent is taken up by umpiring, scoring,

hanging around the pavilion with his pads on, and actually batting (about 3 per cent).

On some occasions the fielding element can achieve a much higher rating, such as when the opposition turns up a man short and requires a substitute fielder.

'Bob, would you like to go out and field for them for a little while?'

On one memorable occasion (which I would in fact prefer to forget) I fielded for the opposition during the whole of Stebbing's innings, since they didn't lose enough wickets for me to be called upon to bat (at No. 11). I then fielded for Stebbing for the whole of the opposition's innings.

I was for some years the Stebbing skipper's favourite choice for the opposition's fielding sub, presumably because I complained less bitterly than the other obvious choices. But this chapter came to an end in a rather dramatic fashion, when I managed to cling on to a running, diving catch on the edge of the mid-wicket boundary. Unfortunately, the ball had just been struck by the skipper himself.

He was less than gracious about it in the pub afterwards:

'I bet you wouldn't 'ave 'ung on to the bugger if you'd been fieldin' for us.'

He never picked me for the opposition again.

The characteristics of the outfield have much to do with the techniques of fielding in village cricket. It's not much good following the old tenets of feet together and hands behind the ball – one has to be ready to move swiftly, and instinctively, in all directions at once as the leather skids off a cowpat, leaps from a pothole, cannons off a molehill and rears from a tuft of couch grass like a striking cobra.

Some fielders may be seen nowadays walking forwards as the bowler starts his run-up. These, I'm afraid, are TV-sated impostors.

You can always tell a genuine village cricketer in the field.

As the bowler starts his run, he will begin to walk backward.

Then there are catches. The steepling ones are the worst. They are normally produced by a powerful tonker, who is aiming for the chestnut grove on the far side of the petrol station. But he gets a thick edge. The ball rises almost vertically to what seems a thousand feet.

You've got plenty of time to study it as it gets smaller and smaller and then, menacingly, bigger and bigger. You look around for a neighbouring fielder, hope to hear someone shout 'Mine!' Then you realize you are all alone, right underneath it.

You assess where it is going to drop, and conclude accurately that it will be right down your gullet, provided you do not move. There are cries of 'Yours, Bob!'

As it descends from a bank of grey scudding cloud you try to keep your eye on it, but it hangs, drifts in the air currents, wobbles about. You circle under it, warily at first, then with increasing panic like a headless fowl. It suddenly falls like a burnt-out rocket. You make a despairing lunge. It bruises your finger-tips. The batsmen have already crossed for two and are going for a third. You hurl the ball at the wicket, hoping to make amends by running one out, but the throw is wild. The bowler grunts with exasperation.

Perhaps the worst experience of all is when you've had a bad run with the bat – three ducks on the trot – and no catch has come your way for a couple of months. Then, as you stand at mid-on, the batsman scoops up a dolly straight at you.

There is no need to move. The catch blossoms, presents itself like a bunch of grapes. The batsman gives a shout of frustration and makes for the pavilion.

You grab at it, a shade too early . . . your fingers close in front of it . . . the ball raps your knuckles and bobbles to the turf.

The batsman returns and cheerfully knocks off the runs required to win.

You get dressed quickly in the silent changing-room afterwards, and go home, missing the pub session. Your wife, reading your expression, knows exactly what has happened as soon as you enter the kitchen.

'Oh no, not again?'

'I'm afraid so.'

You decide to give up the game altogether, take up birdwatching, look up the Essex Naturalists' Trust in the phone book.

By the following week you've decided to give it one more try. And you actually get a knock and notch up about 18, manage to lift one over the chapel wall . . . and when you go out to field you hang on to a snorter.

And you start all over again.

Some village cricketers are able to function well into

their senior citizenship (see Elderly Players), since the game does not necessarily require a peak of physical fitness. But it is the fielding element which eventually reveals the slowing of reflexes, the stiffening of muscles, as the multitudinous hours in the White Hart crowd together and stake their claim.

When I passed forty I began to wonder why drives which I would normally intercept with ease were beginning to streak past me. I tried a few experimental exercises, and discovered that my lowest reach petered out some six inches from the ground. But I managed to compensate for this by developing some fancy footwork, which in turn gave rise to some original repartee, such as: 'Ey, Bob, where are you goin' ter stick it in the net?'

A few years later I became uncomfortably aware that when I fielded a ball on the boundary a younger fielder would materialize, halfway to the wicket, in order to collect my throw and pass it on to the wicketkeeper.

When I reached fifty I used to field at mid-off, considered a safe hiding-place for the unfleet of foot.

Once a batsman drove the ball past me, and I turned and trundled after it. But when I was a couple of yards from where it had come to rest the lithe form of a sixth-form sibling sprinted past me, and plucked it from my grasp. He had come from somewhere in the region of the third-man boundary.

I had a quiet word with him afterwards, concerning territorial rights.

Fund-raising

Cricket clubs, like almost everything else, are becoming more and more expensive to run, while cricketers are becoming increasingly lazy.

Nowadays a local contractor has to be hired to cut the grass. New gear must be frequently acquired, since contemporary cricketers tend to protest vigorously at having to use batting gloves with the webbing rotted by seasons of sweat, strapless pads speckled with moss, or bats which carry more bandages than a motorway casualty.

Then there is insurance, which is a necessary item, just in case some careless oaf gets his finger trapped while trying to start the motor-mower, or a spectator's baby gets a mouthful of leather which has just emerged from the meat of the bat.

These expenses must be met by continuous fund-raising activities. In the old days village clubs used to raise money the hard way, through organizing rummage sales and dances in the village hall – or in the case of Stebbing, weekly bingo sessions, which eventually collapsed when the caller was taken to hospital, suffering from chronic boredom.

After that came the sponsorship craze, sponsored walks and runs, and for the children variations such as sponsored teddy bears' picnics with special prizes for those who could pull their neighbour's golliwog to pieces in the fastest time.

But nobody really wants to exercise themselves too much raising money which they are not going to spend for themselves, and in recent years a variety of fund-raising techniques have been developed which vary from the soft option to straight piracy.

You begin with the basics, the annual subscription paid by the playing members, now running at around £10 per year. Even this requires a strenuous effort from the treasurer in digging it out of reluctant pockets.

Then there are the contributions of presidents and vice-presidents. There are also raffles: I have had more books of tickets stuck under my nose in my cricket career than runs have flowed from my reluctant bat.

I only once had my number shouted, and was

invited to choose between a $\frac{1}{2}$-lb box of dairy milk chocolates and a packet of 20 filter-tipped Benson and Hedges. I chose the chocolates. Over the period, they cost me £127.

About ten years ago large plastic sweet-jars began to appear on the bar counter of the local pub. They contained about a thousand tickets costing 10p each. You bought a ticket and scraped off three small panels to reveal facsimilies of playing-cards. If the value added up to any number between 16 and 21 you won a prize of up to a fiver. There were supposed to be three fiver-winning tickets in each jar, but I never heard of anybody finding one. I once drew a ticket with a winning score of 16. The prize was a free ticket.

More recently this brand of extortion gave way to a

much more efficient one called the 'Hundred Club'. The idea is that a hundred people pay a tenner for the privilege of belonging, and their names would go into a monthly draw for mouth-watering prizes of up to £100.

This technique seems to have evolved around the old W. C. Fields dictum: 'Never give a sucker an even break.'

Stebbing once raised a hefty sum for the club funds by running a stall at the local Elizabethan Fayre. A set of ancient stocks were borrowed, and a quartet of volunteer cricketers took turns to be locked into them and pelted with bags of flour by hordes of enthusiastic visitors.

Whether by accident or design, the 'volunteers' comprised the gang of four.

Ground-work

The annual general meeting of a village cricket club usually takes place in the local pub about the end of March. Some dozen members will attend – about half the playing complement – who will sit huddled in their anoraks against the radiators, rabbiting to each other, while the business of the meeting is going on.

The final item of the agenda will be the organization of a working party for the forthcoming season. The chairman will explain that before the season begins the square has to be repaired from the ravages of the previous one, the pavilion needs six new windows (pushed out during the winter by marauding yobbos), the tea-hut needs a yard or two of felt to stop the rain coming in, and the toadstools really ought to be removed from the walls of the ladies' toilets.

A date will be set for the working party to commence operations (usually three weeks before the first game of the season), and every member present at the AGM will enthusiastically promise to turn up at the ground at 11.00 a.m. on the appropriate Sunday morning.

In the event only five members appear. These will comprise the gang of four (which usually includes the chairman) and a gang-of-seven member who has taken it upon himself to supervise all work on the ground.

It was Dennis who performed this role for Stebbing.

The four of us would tug the heavy roller up and back under his earnest supervision. He would stand behind us as we scratched and scraped away at the dead grass with rakes, occasionally stopping one of us in mid-scrape to demonstrate how to use the implement correctly.

His eyes and ears were everywhere. I once noticed a big clump of plantain weeds growing on the wicket, right on a good length. So I found an old dinner fork in the equipment hut and began gently lifting them. Dennis was standing over me in seconds.

'No, no, you can't take them out now,' he said. 'You'll have to wait until the autumn 'fore you can take them out.'

I decided to cut some turf by the boundary in order to repair the deep scars of the bowlers' footmarks. Dennis didn't approve.

'You can't lay turf this time o' year. That won't have time to settle.'

So I collected a barrowload of molehill earth, and used it to fill the holes, into which I first scattered some grass-seed.

Dennis was peering over my shoulder.

'That en't no good. That won't grow from underneath this time o' year. You'll have to put that on the top.'

'But if I put the seed on top the birds will eat it,' I protested.

Dennis wagged his head with scorn at such ignorance.

'No, no ... birds don't eat grass seed ... not this time o' year.'

I decided I had urgent business elsewhere. As I climbed into the car I saw a flock of finches descend on the wicket and tuck into their providential meal.

Insects

I've often been told that the fastest I've ever been seen to move on a cricket field was during a match against Great Waltham, when a wasp got trapped inside my shirt.

Insects have always been an intermittent cricketing problem. Gnats and midges are a particular nuisance, especially on low-lying meadows. Thunderbugs, which seem to be peculiar to East Anglia, are perhaps the worst. These are microscopic flying beetles which breed in the growing corn and emerge in their millions whenever the sun happens to shine. They don't bite, but they land on the skin, creep up the nostrils and into ears, and wriggle and niggle and diggle away until the host is driven to the borders of insanity.

Also, it seems, special to the Stebbing area is a species of short, squat dung-fly. They pose no immediate threat, but they will gather in a steadily growing cluster over a fielder's head, and dart about in a menacing fashion. You wonder what they have in mind, and why they have chosen you.

Whenever I've been selected by a cluster of dung-flies I have followed a specific course of action. At the end of the over, when the field changes round, I will approach another fielder and engage him in conversation. Then, as the bowler impatiently waits for me to take up my position so that he can bowl, I'll shout 'Sorry', and race across the pitch. The dung-flies, caught off guard by this tactic, will inevitably be left dancing over the head of the fielder I've just been talking to.

But I suppose the British shouldn't complain too much about the insect peril.

While I was on a recent visit to Canada I decided to try for a trout on the banks of a beautiful pine-fringed lake.

I had hardly got my line in before I was engulfed by swarms of vicious bloodsuckers – horseflies, deerflies, blackflies, mosquitoes – and I narrowly escaped being eaten alive before I got back to the car.

I realized soon afterwards why the game of cricket has never really caught on in that part of the Commonwealth.

Local Conditions

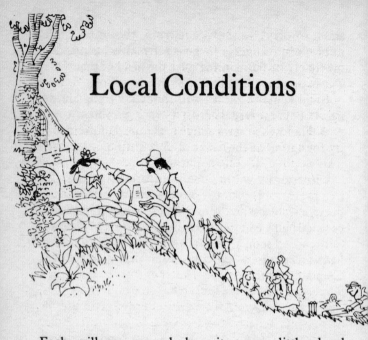

Each village ground has its own little local peculiarities which visiting players must quickly get accustomed to, since the home side will invariably try to turn them to their own advantage.

The Stebbing ground has a flat wicket, but the outfield tilts appreciably, and at different angles, on either side. For a good many years there was also a deep sandpit on the boundary, right behind the wicket, and I was privileged to be present on the celebrated occasion when the village constable, running backward to get under a swirling catch, disappeared into it.

The wicket must always be carefully assessed. I have played on pitches which resembled anything from gluepots to mountain-sides with acne. Great Canfield used to play on a thin mown strip in the centre of a meadow of tall, lush grass. The farmer who owned it insisted on harvesting a hay crop, and the outfield couldn't be cut until the end of June. Early games were inevitably high-scoring. Shots which would normally earn a single sometimes made four or five, as three fielders desperately searched for the ball.

The pitch at Little Bardfield has always been bone-hard, and in a dry season pitted and scarred like a grenade range. Since the club also boasted Robbo, the quickest bowler the area had thrown up for years, visiting clubs were always hard-pressed to find a team.

At Stamborne when I last played there the boundary at one end was marked by an electrified fence, and there was a bull on the other side of it.

Sometimes conditions will be improvised to suit the home side. When a team possesses a good tweaker visiting batsmen will often find a suspicious patch on a length just outside the off-stump, where the grass is always greener. There are some grounds where local conditions are beyond even the home team's control. At Hatfield Heath deep fielders are at serious risk from traffic using the public road which runs through the outfield. At Hatfield Broad Oak a huge cedar of Lebanon stands guard at square-leg, some thirty yards from the wicket.

The Kelvedon ground adjoins a seed merchant's nursery, and its most interesting feature is a rank of large glasshouses, just beyond the boundary, backward of square-leg. They are all of a hundred and twenty yards from the wicket, but look invitingly nearer, and have posed a clear temptation to numerous visiting batsmen down the years, who have sacrificed their wickets in vainglorious attempts to breach them.

I recall an innings I played there with Big Tony. He had gone in at No. 4 and – unusually – spent about six overs quietly playing himself in. But then a cascade of wickets fell. As I arrived at the wicket, batting at No. 9, Tony begged me to try to stay there.

I realized what he had in mind.

He opened his shoulders in the next over and clouted three sixes. The first two were rangefinders. The third came down on the roof of the nearest glasshouse and racketed about inside like a ping-pong ball.

Infected by this exuberance, I took a wild poke at my next ball, which shaved the stumps. Tony walked down the wicket for a disapproving lecture. I quietly played the over out.

During the next he rifled a couple of fours through the off-side, as if for practice, then whacked a towering hook which smashed through one side of the target, out of the other, and through a couple more, while a demented nurseryman capered among the flying splinters.

Big Tony survived for two more overs. We had put on 68 together. Tony had scored 67. There was one leg-bye.

Nerves

These are things which affect most batsmen while they are waiting to go out and bat, and frequently blight their performance.

Actors are known to suffer from the same condition prior to going on, but at least they know roughly *when* their performance is due to start. Batsmen, on the other hand, are obliged to wait for an indeterminate period before they take the stage, and the longer they wait the more serious the nervous condition. The symptoms are usually a racing pulse, a growing sense of nausea in the region of the gut and a dry mouth which if left to dry long enough assumes the characteristics of a gorilla's armpit.

If the batsman is obliged to wait with his pads on for more than half an hour he is normally reduced to the condition of frog-spawn, and this state will accompany him on to the field of play and last for at least a couple of overs, which are seldom survived.

I have tried a number of remedies over the years. The most effective in my experience are taking a series of huge breaths while walking to the wicket in order to slow down the furious heartbeat rate, and chewing peppermints while waiting to bat for the purpose of moistening the mouth.

Nothing else seems to work.

On one occasion, after a series of four ducks on the trot, I filled a large Coca-cola bottle with gin and dry vermouth and left it in the glove compartment of the car. While waiting to bat I sneaked out and took a deep swig every now and again. But Albie and Merv were grafting away, and it was about forty minutes before I got to the crease, by which time the bottle was empty.

I felt fine as I took guard and I knocked up an exuberant 37 before I played over the top of a full-pitched one.

Next time I played I went through the same performance, but snicked a catch to second slip first ball. I never repeated the experiment again, although in retrospect I regret not having given it a fair trial.

There are such people as nerveless cricketers, but

these should be regarded with deep suspicion once they are identified.

They usually turn out to be psychotic.

It's always useful to keep an eye on a batsman who is waiting to go in. If he gets through fifteen fags in twenty minutes, there's nothing wrong with him.

Presidency

This is a non-elective position, filled by invitation of the committee. The president does not turn up at committee meetings, and has nothing to do with the running of the club. (He would make himself unpopular if he tried.) He is required to raise a side during the season to play the village team (The President's Eleven), but his main function is to put his hand in his pocket, which needs to be copious enough to stand the strain.

Until about twenty years ago the local vicar would often fill this role, but since the clergy seems to be getting less and less pecunious nowadays, it is more frequently occupied by a local businessman.

There are usually, in addition to the president, about a dozen vice-presidents. These posts are also filled by invitation, but carry little or no distinction. The incumbents are simply required to donate a tenner a year to the club's funds, for the privilege of having their names printed on the back of the fixture card.

Scorers

A disappearing breed. Until a few years ago most
village sides had their regular scorer who would
appear at home and away matches, logging the overs,
runs, leg-byes and ducks with remorseless accuracy.
For many years the Stebbing scorer was Perce, a

cadaverous man who seemed to purchase his entire wardrobe from an Army surplus store. He performed his duties with cynical humour, always informing the batsmen who complained they weren't out that if they had any doubts in the matter they should consult the scorebook. When an umpire miscounted the balls in an over, and allowed one or two more than the statutory half-dozen, Perce would always consider that the additional ones were unsignalled no-balls, and add them to the score accordingly. (Always provided, of course, that his own side was batting.) I don't think he had ever played the game in his life; one just couldn't imagine him walking out to the wicket.

After his retirement from the scene we decided to try our raffle-ticket seller, Old Jim, in the role. On the first occasion he was entrusted with the scorebook he arrived late from a long pub session. Jim's obsession was rum and blackcurrant, and he appeared with his lips stained crimson by the supportive beverage, like an ancient drag queen.

We were playing Stamborne that day. I had a useful knock, scoring about 25, including a couple of leg-glances to the boundary. As I returned to the pavilion I noticed that my score was lacking eight runs on the scoreboard. I questioned Jim about the two missing boundaries.

'Them was leg-byes,' he insisted.

'No, they weren't. I tickled them round the corner with the bat.'

'Well, I didn't see no bloody umpire's signal,' Jim said. And that was the end of the matter.

Nowadays the scorer is usually a member of the batting side's gang of four, or somebody's girl-friend

(for as long as the relationship lasts) or a schoolboy
hoping to earn himself a game in the event of one of
the players failing to turn up.

Small Boys

It's always a good idea to break in young cricketers at an early age, but this has been known to be overdone, so that a team short of players – perhaps during the harvest season – may field two or three 8-to-10-year-olds at the bottom of the batting order.

The normal practice of the opposition is to serve these nippers with a succession of donkey drops and wait until they miss a straight one. But it can be embarrassing if the scores are close, since these siblings are quite capable of tonking the odd boundary off loose bowling. In such circumstances it is unfortunately necessary to bring on the quicker bowlers to sew the game up before it gets out of hand.

Even so, matters can go sadly awry. In one match against Aythorpe Roding the opposition needed three to win and the last batsman, a pink-cheeked primary schoolboy, was all that stood in our way – he'd already knocked up 14 from one over of rubbish bowling. So the skipper brought back Malc with explicit instructions to finish it.

The first three balls shaved the wicket. The fourth, pitched a bit short, sped to the boundary off the boy's ear. But the pain was quickly submerged as the youngster was carried into the pavilion to the rapturous applause of his team-mates.

'Star' Team Matches

These are functions in which prominent people from the entertainment world form a cricket team to play village sides in areas close to London, in order to raise money for charities.

The results are usually disappointing, since entertainers are apt to be booked at five minutes' notice, and hard professionalism always triumphs over the charitable instinct, so that the team finally emerges as someone like Jimmy Savile (Capt.) supported by three or four West Ham reserve footballers, one or two hoofers from *The Dancing Years* which has just finished its run at Hornchurch, and a couple of buglers from the Romford Silver and Marching Band who are alleged to be able to bowl. The host team are telephoned a couple of hours before the game is due to start and asked if they can supply a couple of lads to make up the shortfall. The visitors are always optimistically described in the pre-match publicity as an 'All-Star Eleven'.

Stebbing, however, has a built-in, genuine All-Stars game every season.

Some twenty years ago Richard, a leading agent in the entertainment world, acquired the local manor, Stebbing Park, as his week-end pad.

Rumours soon began to circulate thickly. David Frost had taken to dropping in by helicopter for business conferences. The cigar-smokers lounging in the back of the Silver Ghost seen cruising through the High Street had been positively identified as the Two Ronnies. The bland, tweed-suited character who had stopped off for lunch at the White Hart had signed his cheque with the name of Russell Harty.

Within a few years Richard had brought a team down composed of his clients and associates to play a one-day match against the village side. The fixture has since become an annual event.

The scenario is something like this:

The match is due to start at 11.00 a.m. At about a quarter past the early arrivals from the home team are joined by the first All-Stars, straggling across the footpath from the Park.

A roped enclosure has been erected in front of the pavilion with ranks of chairs borrowed from the Congregational Hall, and a fresh-painted notice which says, 'Members and Guests Only'. Throughout the day, nobody takes any notice of the notice.

The game gets under way at 11.40. Stebbing lose the toss and get put in to bat. The home team is not perhaps at its strongest, containing a mixture of its best younger players and those older ones still powerful enough to demand a place for this particular match, including myself.

Richard's team is captained by Tim Rice (author of that immortal line, 'Don't cry for me, Argentina'), who clearly knows his cricket from the way he sets his field, even moving a tense-looking, bearded young man from deep square to mid-wicket between overs. He is the only man in his side who carries an air of authority, apart from the wicketkeeper, who used to play for Middlesex, and has a demeanour of wry and cynical amusement.

It is mid-June, but unusually for the time of year the weather is coming from a huge ridge of high pressure centred over the Urals, and while the skies are clear enough to permit the occasional glint of sunlight a vicious breeze is leaking in from the Arctic.

The score mounts fairly quickly, but wickets fall regularly, largely through impetuous strokes. Rice keeps changing the bowling, and it is clear that he intends to give everyone a bowl, so that the quality of the deliveries varies between the wild pacey stuff of a couple of young pop singers through the friendly offerings of Richard Stilgoe to the dull but workmanlike stuff of Rice himself. Lunch has been set for 1.15. At one o'clock we are 82-7. I am due to bat at No. 10, and I sit on the pavilion veranda with my pads on. But by lunch-time no further wicket has fallen, so I take them off again.

A buffet lunch of superior quality is served on Richard's lawn beside the water-lily pond. Wine begins to circulate freely. The Stebbing cricketers congregate at one side of the lawn, the exotic visitors cluster together at the other. There is a distinct 'them and us' sort of atmosphere.

Afterwards we wander back to the ground and get on with the business again. As soon as I've finished strapping the pads on our skipper announces he's decided to declare.

The All-Stars open their innings. From the beginning the batsmen appear extremely shaky and lacking in sound technique, most of the runs coming off the edge, from cross-batted swings. One of the early batsmen is a pop singer whose group has a record in the charts, but nobody is quite sure who it is, or what it is.

Stumps are rattled regularly. Stilgoe comes out to bat, looking like Mike Gatting, until he squares up to the bowling and the resemblance ends. After three balls he cocks up a simple catch to mid-on, where I happen to be fielding. As he passes me on the way back to the pavilion he complains, 'It's the only game I get all season and you have to catch me out third ball!'

His successor comes out to bat, and a few balls later knocks the ball in my direction and goes for a quick single. His partner is reluctant, and there is a horrible mix-up in the middle of the pitch. I've got bags of time to flip the ball to the wicketkeeper, but Stilgoe's remarks have inculcated a deep feeling of guilt, so I juggle the ball like a burning ember, drop it, pick it up, juggle with it again, until at last they scamper back. Sighs of relief all round. Shouts of 'Well done, Bob!'

The innings firms up appreciably at this point. Tim Rice manages to stay there, while the man who used to play for Middlesex rattles up about forty in a laconic, professional style.

It is now well into the afternoon, and the roped enclosure is filling up. Esther Rantzen materializes in billowing blue chiffon like a junior version of the Queen, her celebrated teeth chattering with cold. She wraps herself gratefully in a sheepskin parka proffered by an acolyte.

Someone identifies two young men as Hinge and Bracket, a well-known drag act, although none of the Stebbing cricketers can quite believe it. A refugee from the King's Singers draws himself a pint from the barrel placed at the entrance to the pavilion. As Ernie, the village farrier, follows suit, someone with an autograph book asks if he is Jasper Carrott.

Ernie has never heard the name before, but signs the book nevertheless, although he has to ask how to spell it.

The All-Stars innings leaks to its end. There is a twenty-minute break for refreshments before Stebbing go in to bat again, thirty-one runs ahead on

the first innings. At this point the Controller of BBC 1 Television decides he has had enough for the day, and hands over to his nephew, who has been lurking around the pavilion all day, waiting for the call.

Stebbing's second innings gets away to a brisk start, the Muscadet slurping around the heavy lunch having begun to slow the All-Star reflexes.

A simple catch goes down. Rice patiently resets the field: 'Come in a bit, Andrew; Richard, would you like to drop back a bit? Good. Thanks!' But after a few overs the nephew is given a bowl and takes three quick wickets. There is a buzz of speculation around the pavilion as to why he wasn't put on during the first innings.

It is soon time for tea. The fielders straggle in, talking shop with less enthusiasm now.

The tea itself is something of an occasion in its own right. For this special event the Stebbing tea-ladies have made a special effort. The sandwiches – tongue and cucumber, egg and lettuce, cream cheese and cress, ham and tomato – are soft as feather pillows, but this is far from all. There are flake-pastry sausage rolls, vol-au-vent, biscuits with olives in the middle, and all this is just for starters. Beyond them are the ranks of cakes lined up for afters – thick chocolate cakes with thick chocolate icing, cherry cake, madeira cake, banbury cake, seedcake, treacle tart, apple dumpling, sponge roll, peanut nuggets, ginger biscuits, Scotch shortbread.

There is much more of this than twenty-two cricketers can consume, and before long plates of goodies and trays of teacups begin to circulate among the guests, visitors, and camp-followers.

These include a coterie of attractive women, wives and mistresses of the All Star players, squatting on mohair car rugs on the grass in the lee of the pavilion. They have congregated into two specialized groups – those who are purely and outrageously sexy, and those who are sexy and intellectual with it. The ladies of both these groups will giggle and smirk at each other when presented with these mountains of calories. One by one they will pick the walnut off the top and chew it, lick the icing reflectively, then swallow the rest in four bites.

The tea-break lasts for almost an hour. There are only two more wickets to fall before it is my turn to bat, but I've long since given up hope of getting a knock. My pessimism is justified. After tea our skipper decides that a lead of 96 is sufficient, and once again declares. We troop out to field for the last time.

There is an atmosphere of weariness, of moral flatulence, which is reflected in the play. Our bowling is not worth a fart. Fielders stop balls with their feet, or not at all. The nephew, promoted to open the innings, cracks a couple of smart boundaries, and is then bowled between his legs by a fortuitous squatter. I stand at backward square leg, feeling not so much that I've been playing cricket all day but rather eating and drinking, with the certain knowledge that there is a good deal more of the latter to come.

Despite the shoddy bowling – or perhaps because of it – the All-Stars innings disintegrates at an accelerating pace. Stilgoe tries hard, stays there for two or three overs, then cocks up a dolly to silly mid-off and departs, whacking his pads with his bat in frustration. Rice swings across the line of a straight chinaman and is bowled. When the Middlesex man comes in it is a quarter to six, and pub opening time beckons. He clouts a couple of sixes, and is then caught on the square-leg boundary. The All-Stars are still thirty-six runs short. The last pair niggle and fiddle around for twenty minutes, giving the impression that they would like to get out, but don't quite know how to.

The bowler at last gets one on the wicket as a first flurry of rain sweeps across the field.

In the White Hart afterwards jugs of ale are filled and refilled and passed around dangerously through the crush of bodies. The publican has made his own contribution to the occasion and the bar counter is cluttered with dishes of snacks – nuts, crisps, cockles and mussels, prawns, beef sandwiches, huge slices of pork pie. The Stebbing cricketers edge away from Esther Rantzen, afraid she is going to ask them an embarrassing question: 'Excuse me . . . do you wear pyjamas when you go to bed . . . or a nightshirt . . . or nothing at all?'

But the pub session lasts for only half an hour. Richard the host has organized a dinner for his guests at Easton barn, a rural restaurant some three miles distant, to which the Stebbing club's 'officers' – i.e., president, chairman and committee – are also invited. So it is not long before the All-Star contingent melt away like a well-drilled infantry platoon, followed by their camp-followers and the Stebbing officers.

At the Barn Restaurant, a genuine Elizabethan oak-beamed relic tarted up a little, the lighting is subdued, red cloths on the tables – about eight of them, each seating a dozen. The one in the middle has been set aside for the Stebbing officers. We sit there waiting for the asparagus soup, feeling like a coach party en route to a matinée performance of *No Sex Please*, *We're British*, which has somehow got mixed up with the annual awards jamboree of the British Academy of Film and Television Arts.

Our host Richard makes a speech. Stebbing's president, Alan, makes a shorter one. Then the jaws of comics, composers, musicians, assorted television personalities, minstrels and their ladies, champ and chatter over the roast beef, Yorkshire pudding, unfrozen sprouts, horseradish sauce in packets followed by tinned peach Melba with whipped cream.

90

There is more wine, red, white and rosé, and later with the coffee, brandy and cigars.

The Cambridge Buskers, a couple of lively performers with flute and concertina, entertain us with renditions of Mozart sonatas and traditional jigs. They have come a long way since they performed for tourists outside King's College Chapel.

As midnight approaches the tables thin. Snorts and skids of Mercs and Jags outside as the All-Stars head for the M11.

Waitresses in scarlet pinafores come to collect the bottles. It's only another week before real cricket starts again.

Transport Arrangements

Transport to away games is usually by car-sharing, with three or four players travelling in each of several vehicles. This can be a perilous business and it is wise to avoid being a fellow-traveller in the wagon of the kind of cricketer – by no means rare – who likes to drink for about two and a half hours at the opposition's local, and then attempt to break his personal speed-record back to the village.

After one game against King John Old Boys the car I was returning home in stopped at the roadside so that the occupants could respond to the call of nature behind the adjacent hedge. While we were engrossed in this activity another carful of fellow-cricketers drew up behind, and one of its more inebriated occupants climbed into the driving-seat of the empty vehicle and started the engine.

As we were adjusting our dress we were startled to see our transport receding over the brow of the hill.

Treasurer

The ideal incumbent of this post will be a man of indeterminate age with a prison haircut, who wears a fawn raincoat over bib-and-brace overalls with a collar and tie, winter and summer.

He can frequently be seen riding through the village on a vintage ladies' bicycle with an old-fashioned chainguard. He has no knowledge of accountancy or bookkeeping, and will present his accounts at the annual general meeting in the form of a collection of scruffy bits of paper covered with illegible handwriting. To questions such as: 'Ow much 'ave we got in the kitty then, Syd?' he will reply, 'Can't you bloody read?' The outstanding feature of his personality is an unremitting parsimony. Beside him Scrooge is a mere amateur.

But this quality is absolutely essential as a counterweight to another archetypal committee member, the compulsive spender.

This member is usually a lean and lank carpet salesman with a glib line of patter which if unchecked can be all too persuasive. His compulsion is confined exclusively to the spending of other people's money. On the home front he is the sort of man who requires his children to present him with a weekly account of how they spend their pocket-money.

A cunning chairman will always try to play the

treasurer off against the compulsive spender. He will first of all arrange the agenda so that no item will permit the compulsive spender to launch himself on a spending spree. A really unscrupulous chairman will deliberately run the meeting over its allotted span, and will then announce that there's no time for any other business. But a fair-minded chairman will include this final item, always provided that he has confidence that his treasurer can cope with the compulsive spender. The ensuing exchanges will be rather like this:

Chairman. Right. Any other business? Only you'll have to be quick, because the bar's closing in five minutes.

Comp. Spender. Well, Mr Chairman, according to the accounts, we've got £432 in the kitty and I think we ought to do something with it. I'd like to propose that we lay electricity on to the pavilion.

Treas. Whaffor?

Comp. Spender. Well . . . electric lights, of course . . . and we could have an electric kettle in the tea-hut.

Treas. What you want electric light for? Everyone's gorn 'ome before that gets dark.

Comp. Spender. Yes, well, I suppose that might be true in the early part of the season. But towards the end of September . . .

Treas. I suppose you'll be wantin' a bloody bar an' dancin' girls next. We ain't Bishop's Stortford, y'know. Look, if you want to spend some money, the Hayter mower's packed up, and that's goin' ter cost forty quid to sort out. Then you've got your insurance, that went up double last season. I've just 'ad to order a gallon o' weed-killer for the nettles, that was fourteen quid, and we ain't got the bill for the felt for the pavilion roof yet awhile. I got a bill 'ere for twenty-seven quid for new bat 'andles, an' another for new blades – that's another thirty-six. D'you know 'ow much a new pack of 'alf a dozen cricket balls cost nowadays? . . . well, I'll tell yer . . .

Chairman. Right. I declare this meeting closed. And I'll expect to see the lot of you down for work on the ground next Sunday week . . . all right?

Umpires

One has an image of a cantankerous, bucolic elder, tufts of black hair sprouting from his nostrils, squatting on a shooting-stick and radiating disapproval of the events around him.

These personalities certainly used to exist. There was one who played for a neighbouring village (which I decline to identify for obvious reasons) who walked to the wicket in the deliberate but disjointed manner of a turtle on dry land. His approach was direct and simple: allow every appeal by one's own bowlers, reject every appeal by those of the opposition. He was known throughout the area as 'the twelfth man'.

This veteran once nodded asleep on his shooting-stick during a match against Stebbing, and the bowler sent down fourteen deliveries before deciding to wake him up. Our scorer decided that the over must have included eight no-balls, and entered them in the extras column accordingly.

There was also Curly, another opposition umpire, a somewhat corpulent man with a nose like a greenhouse pepper left for seed, who wore a flat tweed cap jammed on top of his glittering dome. He always brought to the game his dog, an overweight cocker spaniel, which was left tied to the pavilion rails during the course of the game, but always managed to wriggle free about half a dozen times over the duration of the proceedings and waddle on to the field to lick its master's boots.

We were playing his team away on one occasion, and Trevor was bowling. The batsman got an edge to one which cracked like an exploding fuse as it glanced off the bat and whacked into the wicketkeeper's hands.

The batsman declined to walk, but instead flicked some imaginary dust from the side of his pad. Curly seemed oblivious to the howls.

After a disbelieving hiatus of about ten seconds Trevor began to make a series of not too polite observations.

Curly turned his head the other way.

'Talk into this ear, bo-oy,' he said. 'I'm stone deaf in the other bugger.'

Trevor spoke very loudly into the lobe which was offered.

'You sure you're not deaf in this bastard too?'

Unfortunately, this is all in the past. I don't know what old buggers like Curly and the Twelfth Man do during the summer week-ends any more, but they are certainly not standing at the wicket. I suspect they are sitting with their feet on the table, watching John Player League cricket on BBC2.

The system is now – and has been for some time – that members of the batting side take turns to do the umpiring, when they are not batting themselves.

For many years, as an established member of the gang of four, batting at about 10 or 11, I would regularly be handed the coat for a duty lasting some hour and three-quarters, before handing over to one of the opening batsmen, long dismissed, so that I could go and get my pads on. I would be trying to find a pair of gloves which matched when tea-time was called, and the skipper declared.

But I eventually rebelled against this exploitation, and when I knew that Stebbing were about to bat I would hide, stretching myself out on the back seat of my car – a clapped-out but commodious Rover – lighting a pipe and turning on the car radio, broadcasting a Test Match or the Wimbledon tennis.

The murmurous voice of the skipper would intrude upon those of the commentators.

'McEnroe serves, deep to the backhand ... Connors across court low over the net...'

'Bob! Anyone seen Bob?'

'And now Kapil Dev comes in to bowl. Tavare

receiving . . . And Kapil Dev bowls . . . and Tavare, defensively and rather suspiciously, prods forward . . .'

'I saw 'im go round the back of the pavilion, and then 'e disappeared.'

'Connors a lob . . . and McEnroe races back . . . and returns it marvellously, deep to the backhand court . . .'

'Pete . . . where's Pete?'

'And Botham a somewhat uncharacteristic forward defensive stroke . . .'

'Peter . . . look, Bob's disappeared . . . would you like to umpire for a little while . . .?'

'Connors a volley . . . comes to the net . . . McEnroe . . . aaaaah!'

'Yeh, I know, but somebody's got to do it.'

'And Willis beats him again outside the off-stump . . . and he stands and glares . . . shrugs his shoulders . . . begins his long walk back . . .'

'Where's Simon? Sime . . .?'

'And Connors a ferocious backhand down the line . . . a clear winner!'

'Oh, Christ, I suppose I'll 'ave to do it myself!'

'Game, set, and match!'

When standing as umpire against one's own batting side impartiality is not always easy to impart. I quickly became accustomed to the recriminations in the pavilion afterwards . . . 'That's the first time I've ever been given out caught to a bumped ball . . .' etc. On the other hand, I've never heard a batsman say something like, 'I was surprised you didn't give me out stumped . . . I thought I was at least a foot out of the crease . . .'

There is also the problem of keeping up with the changing rules of cricket, which are handed down by the moguls at St John's Wood, and take some years to percolate to the grass roots, if they ever reach there at all.

The rule for leg before wicket is a case in point. A batsman is supposed to be out nowadays if he gets his leg in the way of an off-break, without playing a stroke. But what is the situation if you've got a right-hand leg-break bowler bowling over the wicket to a left-hand batsman . . . or a left-hand bowler bowling off-breaks round the wicket to an ambidextrous dwarf who blocks them with his chest?

My golden rule has been always to stand by a decision once it has been made, because however much it may offend the injured party, to change it is likely to arouse the opposition to the point of paranoia.

While I was umpiring in a home match one of Stebbing's best batsmen, Colin, chopped a ball a few yards in front of him and tried to take a quick single. But the opposition's clown, fielding at short mid-on, went for the ball and blundered into him, knocking him flat. He scrambled up and tried to make his ground, but another fielder had tossed the ball to the bowler, who in his excitement trod on the wicket.

My own attention was fixed on the drama in front, but I heard the furniture collapse and raised my finger.

Colin was outraged. 'How can I be run out? 'E didn't even touch the stumps with the ball.'

'I know,' I said. 'But I've got to give you out for obstructing a fielder.'

He did speak to me again . . . after a lapse of about five years.

Unpopular Players

These are nearly always members of the opposition, of course.

Being over-keen is always an unhealthy sign, often observed in bowlers who have been watching too many Test matches on television, so that when they appeal for lbw they will crouch and spread their arms and give a triumphant scream . . . then leap about as if a positive decision has already been taken.

When the umpire fails to collaborate they will roll their eyes with disbelief, mutter and grunt with exasperation, sometimes lie prostrate on the pitch.

Then they walk back to bowl again, shouting to their team-mates, 'I suppose I'll have to hit the bloody stumps!'

Fielders can also be guilty of this kind of misbehaviour. You will see one take a dollied catch, shouting 'Mine!' when nobody else is near him, then toss it high in the air after he's pouched it ... a performance which suggests he's just got rid of Geoffrey Boycott, rather than a Little Dunmow tail-ender.

Paradoxically, it is usually the good cricketers who bring the game into disrepute in this fashion, largely through an excess of self-appreciation. On the other hand, this is perhaps logical. A regular member of a team's gang of four, behaving like a prima donna, would hardly expect to get another game for the rest of the season.

These manifestations of self-love need to be quickly extinguished in case they become contagious and create an unpopular team. One batsman, playing for High Roding, knocked up about eighty, and shouted to the pavilion, 'Ow many do I need for me 'undred?' At the end of the over his skipper declared.

A Stebbing player (new to the village, and playing his first game) knocked up a hundred, and was later put on to bowl. He had a confident shout for lbw turned down, and went through the familiar routine of gasping and fuming.

A couple of overs later, as he ran up to bowl, he attempted to run out the batsman as he was backing up.

The umpire dismissed the appeal. He looked appalled.

'What d'you mean, not out? He was at least a yard out of his crease.'

'I know. But 'ow would you like it if I gave you out, just because some silly bugger whipped the bails off when 'e was supposed to be bowlin'?'

The umpire stuck his pipe back in his mouth.

'Anyway, it was a no-ball, now I come to think about it.'

One of the least popular cricketers in my experience was George, who opened the batting for Wendon's Ambo.

George, approaching middle age, had recently stepped down from club cricket, and his approach was typical of this background. He would spend the first hour playing himself in, and start scoring when the bowlers were tired and frustrated. His attitude was that of a professional among amateurs.

On one occasion when I was the opposing skipper he began his knock in typical fashion, and I crowded him with close fielders, hoping to force an error before he got set. In the fifth over Trevor – our nearest approach to a quickie – put one down a bit short of a length which rose sharply and moved in a few inches. George tickled it to the wicketkeeper. He nodded his respects to Trevor and began to walk.

When he had walked twenty yards towards the pavilion the umpire at the bowler's end – one of his team-mates – called out, 'Hey, George, come back! You never touched it.'

George stopped and turned, hope rekindling in his eyes.

'Oh, didn't I? Sorry.'

He walked back to the wicket and took a fresh guard.

I took Trevor off and fed George with rubbish for the rest of the afternoon. He punished it remorselessly, and I don't think he ever got the message, until I put myself on and bowled underarm. But it was too late to make any difference.

He was already transfixed, his photograph in the *Herts and Essex Observer*, under the caption 'Innings of The Week'.

Yet perhaps the pride of place in this gallery should go to Edgar, who opened the batting for High Garrett for years. He was a man of indeterminate age, with the features of an anxious gnome and the physique of a stick insect. He always played for a draw.

In time the whole psychological approach of the team came to be built around him. When the High Garrett skipper won the toss he would put the other side in to bat, and rely on Edgar to make a draw out of it.

To Edgar every ball – full toss, yorker, bouncer, beamer – was the same. He would anchor his right toe on the popping crease, reach forward a couple of yards, and drop a dead bat on it. He was impossible to shift; he never made any runs, or attempted a scoring shot, whatever the state of the game – this was for others. Yet he managed to stamp his personality on a whole generation of cricketers.

Unpopular Teams

The fixture list of the normal village club is based on a mixture of geography and tradition, but is nevertheless subject to a good deal of fluctuation.

The hard core of the list is represented largely by other village sides within a ten-mile radius. Then there are the tourists – teams of old boys from grammar schools, ex-paratroops, West Indian lawyers from the Inns of Court, who play only away fixtures, having no ground of their own. Sometimes these wanderers drift out of existence, leaving a hole to be filled in the fixture list. It is not unknown for a

team to turn up at an away fixture to find another team in the visitors' changing-room. This normally leads to an acrimonious exchange of letters between secretaries, each blaming the other for the balls-up.

On other occasions a contretemps may develop which will lead to cancellation of future fixtures. One such event occurred when Stebbing were playing an away game against a printing-works team.

The home side batted first and scratched 65 runs together. At six-thirty that evening Stebbing were cruising along nicely at 52-3. The opposing skipper then walked on to the field, clicking his fingers. All of the fielding side then walked off. The skipper announced apologetically that he had promised his lads faithfully that they could pack up and go home at half-past six to watch the final of the European Cup on television.

We never played them again.

But it's the new and unknown teams which create the worst problems. Early in the year a number of clubs will advertise for fixtures in the local newspapers. (This in itself is suspicious. Why can't they get anyone to play them?) However, a village-club secretary with one or two gaps in his fixture-list will be tempted to respond. The result can often be disconcerting.

One new club we played for the first time (also the last) was Upshire, a village on the fringe of Epping Forest. (Well into the dangerous commuter fringe.) It was an away game, played on a blustery, unpleasant sort of day, and I was the Stebbing captain on that occasion.

As we arrived the opposition (already changed)

were indulging in organized catching practice. When I shook hands with the opposing skipper – a young blond fellow with a permanent expression of refined disgust – he pointed out that we were already five minutes late (we'd lost our way) and suggested tea should be taken at any time between 4.30 and 5.15, according to the state of the game. I realized that he was trying to keep all his options open, but felt reluctantly obliged to agree, not wishing to poison a new fixture.

We tossed up. I lost. The opposition, of course, batted.

They batted with almost religious intensity. Batsmen given out hung around at the crease, glowering with displeasure, and bumping their bats on the ground before departing. Batsmen due to go in next practised assiduously in the nets. Each scoring stroke drew a ripple of applause from the batsmen sitting in the pavilion.

I noticed that there were no non-playing spectators.

Upshire batted on until 5.15, by which time they had accumulated 192-9. We took tea. In fact there was no tea as such, the hired tea-lady having neglected to appear with the urn.

For half an hour we munched stale Eccles cakes and dog-eared cheese and tomato sandwiches bought from a local grocery store some days earlier. We then went out to bat with an hour and three-quarters to surpass the score which the opposition had amassed in two and a half.

They had their own umpires. To give these worthies their due, they did not respond positively to all the rapturous howling and yelling and leaping which occurred each time a Stebbing batsman was hit on the pad. But they did so often enough to make serious inroads into our batting resources.

On this late September evening it had grown dark by seven o'clock. Vast bellies of black cloud scudded low across the ground. Jumbo jets throbbed invisibly above them as they stacked over Heathrow Airport.

Flurries of heavy rain began to sweep across the field, but neither the umpires nor the fielding side made any move to take shelter.

The match was due to finish at 7.30, but the opposing skipper had enforced the 20-over rule for the last hour's play. 'We always observe it here,' he had said, as we were finishing our tea.

By 7.30 we were 7 wickets down for about 80, but only twelve of the overs had been bowled. Between overs there was a great deal of hithering and thithering of fieldsmen, shouts of encouragement, exhortations to 'keep on your toes'.

At eight o'clock, with three overs to go, we were eight wickets down. But their fast bowlers were close to exhaustion. I was still there. Between balls, I observed bats – the animal kind – darting around a huge chestnut-tree through a haze of rain. In the next over Barry was hit in the chest and departed lbw.

One over to go. I was facing the bowling.

Now, Stebbing cricketers never play for a draw. But in the circumstances, with nine Upshire upstarts crouching within five yards of the bat, I decided to try and see the over out.

The bowling was slow, the ball coming sluggishly off the sodden wicket like a rotten orange out of a dark tunnel. I dead-batted the first five balls down in front of me, safe from the grabbing hands and the floundering bodies.

One ball left. I knew it was all over. I decided to whack it out of the ground as a final gesture of defiance. It took the top edge, flew high, and the silly point, running backward, grabbed it three inches from the ground.

Out of courtesy, we decided to call in at the Upshire pub for a quick drink before returning.

We were quickly surrounded by jubilant, smirking cricketers. The Upshire skipper clapped me on the shoulder.

'I thought we would never get you out.'

'Well, I didn't want to be responsible for someone's suicide.'

Later he came round wagging a collection-box. 'The planners are trying to drive a motorway through the centre of our ground', he explained, 'and we're collecting funds to fight it.'

Someone dropped twopence in the box.

'When is this likely to happen?' asked Barry.

Whitbread Cup

A national competition for village-cricket clubs. Used to be the Haig Cup.

There are rules and regulations, easily bent, which are intended to make this a true village cricket competition. But by the time the contestants reach the quarter-finals you will find that the same teams are involved as last year, and the year before.

These teams will consist of Minor Counties and Lancashire League type cricketers, with only one gang-of-four member (usually recruited because he can speak with the local rustic accent, although he may never have played the game before). The final might just as well be billed as accountants and stockbrokers versus solicitors and architects.

The normal village whose team reaches the final of the Whitbread Cup will be a picturesque dormitory about five miles from a town the size of Romford or Cheltenham. The local council will have built a spanking great sports and recreation centre there, with cricket and football fields, vast pavilion, tennis and badminton courts, bar, restaurant – the lot. And these facilities will attract all the classy cricketers who don't want to get stuck in Romford's second eleven, because they'd much rather play in rustic surroundings. Deputy assistant bank managers, after all, don't always enjoy playing against a continuous diet of junior executives from the Department of Health and Social Services. They'd much prefer to jut their straight bats against the straw-suckers from Tolleshunt D'Arcy.

The Whitbread Cup is basically a forty-over-a-side contest. This is itself foreign to the nature of village cricket, which develops its own cantankerous pace, slow and pastoral for some periods, fast and frenetic at others, whose separate elements are not contrived, but are of an emotional and utterly unpredictable quality.

In a limited-over match, however, an essential technique has to be imposed. There is a need for a cautious beginning, slowly accelerating towards a frenzied climax, while keeping wickets in hand.

Genuine village cricket clubs are simply not geared to this sort of discipline, and react to it with all the acumen of bumble-bees in a greenhouse. At Stebbing, for example, our openers for many years were Merv and Albie, both patient, plodding grafters who needed to get their heads down for an hour before they could begin to castigate the opposition's trundlers – assuming they were still there. When it came to limited-over matches one of them needed to be demoted to about No. 8 in the batting order. But which one? And where was the captain brave enough to take such a revolutionary decision?

What normally happened was that they would put together 27 between them during the first thirty overs, then have a wild fling in response to the anguished cries from the pavilion, and get out. The Stebbing innings would fizzle out at 65-3 with the

team's one genuine match-winning tonker sitting on the veranda chewing his gloves.

There was only one occasion when we actually won a game in this competition, and I seem to remember that on this occasion either Merv or Albie had to go to a wedding, and we beat some bunch from Hertfordshire by a couple of runs. A week or two later our prize arrived – a magnum of Scotch. It went down very sweetly in the changing-room after the next round of the competition.

We lost that one but nobody seemed to mind, which only goes to prove that everything in life has its compensations provided you are prepared to wait until they arrive.

Women's Role

Making the teas is about all, I'm afraid. One strange team we played — I seem to remember they came from Dedham or somewhere — did turn up with a female player, and she wasn't all that bad-looking. She had to put her gear on in someone's car while we all pretended to look the other way.

When she went in to bat I was impressed by her

sound defensive technique for the first couple of overs, although the bowling at that time was pretty straightforward medium-paced up-and-down sort of stuff.

During the third over she succumbed to natural human emotions and took a monumental lunge at one which was only just short of a length.

I was fielding backward of point.

Normally when I get under a high catch it emerges straight from the centre of a blazing sun. On this occasion that problem was behind me and the ball was etched perfectly against a bank of cirro-cumulus like a cherry on a bowl of mashed potatoes.

I contemplated long and fiercely as it reached the apex of its trajectory and began its graceful descent.

Supposing I dropped it . . . and the lady went on to reach her fifty .. or even a ton . . . this would encourage the others. Within a few years every village cricket team would have its feminine complement.

The game would take on a different complexion. Concentrations would waver, disciplines would disintegrate, complications would take place in the long grass behind the pavilion, victories and defeats would no longer be worked out in the crass terms of runs scored and wickets taken.

A lovely prospect beckoned. Unfortunately, my hands had not grabbed a decent catch all season, and they ignored the urgent signals screamed from every nerve-end.

I caught it. I didn't have to move an inch.

Nobody would buy me a pint in the pub afterwards.

For some years we had an annual fixture against 'the ladies'. The men had to bowl left-handed – a surprisingly difficult feat – and most of the ladies' runs were garnered from wides. On one occasion I recall batting in such a match and reaping a welcome harvest from a series of long hops down the leg-side. At the end of the over I was approached by Big Tony, who was batting at the other end. He looked appalled. 'What are you trying to do, win the bloody game?'

The next ball I received I departed, hit wicket, to smirks of relief all round.

In that game the ladies fielded a wicketkeeper with the physical accoutrements of Dolly Parton. While the men were batting a knot of them collected on the boundary behind the wicket, while those at the crease were hard put to watch their front.

But this is not to decry the female sex. Women, after all, are essential participants in the only sport known to society, throughout history, which is actually superior to village cricket.

Young Players

I have played against some village sides which are almost exclusively composed of geriatrics, which in village cricket terms means anyone over thirty-seven. Such sides are always socially congenial in pub-afterwards terms, but there is a clear necessity to encourage young blood in order to perpetuate the species.

The problem with the young is that you normally grab them at about fifteen, when they begin to show promise and even enthusiasm, but two years later they tend to be seduced away from the game, not so much by lascivious young chicks (which would be entirely understandable) but by snarling and snorting Hondas, and automatic gambling machines with supplementary nudging facilities.

Young Stan was such a case. He had played for the first eleven at the local comprehensive before leaving at sixteen, when I first encouraged him, during my term as skipper, to play for Stebbing. This was a socially committed attempt to seduce him away from the gang of yobbos who were accustomed to hanging around my front gate at twilight and kicking in the wooden panels of my fence as soon as darkness had fallen.

Stan was small and slight, even for his age, but he had a natural rhythm as a bowler, and could smack it down on a shilling. At the height of his brief career he took 6-27 against our local rivals, Lindsell. But at the next home game he was jeered throughout by the local yobbos, squatting on the grass beside the chapel wall. He bowled atrociously, and got a duck.

It was his last appearance. At the next home game I found myself being jeered every time I fielded the ball, by the self-same bunch of yobbos.

Except that this time young Stan was among them.